West Midlands
RAILS IN THE 1980s

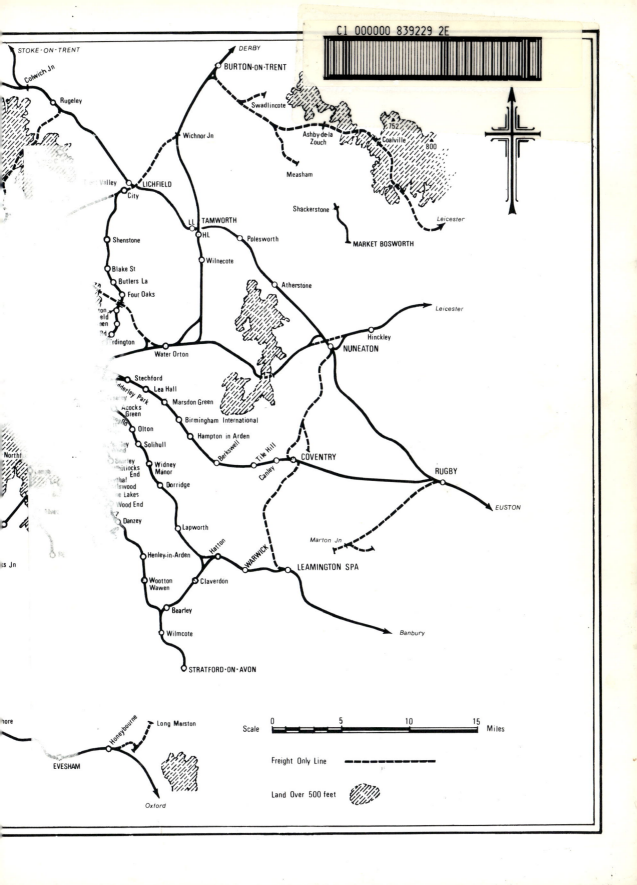

STOKE·ON·TRENT

Colwich Jn

Rugeley

DERBY

BURTON·ON·TRENT

Swadlincote

Wichnor Jn

Ashby-de-la Zouch

Measham

Coalville

752

800

Valley

LICHFIELD

City

Shackerstone

Leicester

LL TAMWORTH

HL

MARKET BOSWORTH

Shenstone

Polesworth

Wilnecote

Blake St

Atherstone

Butlers La

Four Oaks

Leicester

Hinckley

rdington

Water Orton

NUNEATON

Stechford

Lea Hall

nderley Park

Marsdon Green

cocks Green

Birmingham International

Olton

Hampton in Arden

ley

Solihull

Berkswell

Tile Hill

COVENTRY

Northf

Shirley

Widney Manor

Canley

hitlocks End

RUGBY

swood

Dorridge

EUSTON

e Lakes

Wood End

Danzey

Lapworth

Marton Jn

Henley-in-Arden

Hatton

WARWICK

Wootton Wawen

Claverdon

LEAMINGTON SPA

Bearley

Wilmcote

Banbury

STRATFORD·ON·AVON

ks Jn

nore

Honeybourne

Long Marston

EVESHAM

Oxford

Scale

0   5   10   15

Miles

Freight Only Line

Land Over 500 feet

West Midlands

RAILS IN THE 1980s

John Glover

LONDON

IAN ALLAN LTD

Contents

First published 1984

ISBN 0 7110 135

© Ian Allan Ltd 1984

Published by Ian Allan Ltd, Shepperton, Surrey;
and printed by Ian Allan Printing Ltd at their works
at Coombelands in Runnymede, England.

Introduction

'We're moving London (or Manchester or Liverpool)
closer to the Heart of England' proclaimed the
advertisement hoardings. The occasion was the
completion of the original London Midland Region
main line electrification scheme, which from
5 March 1967 brought Coventry, Birmingham and
Wolverhampton into the electric InterCity network.
Fifteen years later, this volume takes a pictorial look
at these and other rail services today in an area
loosely defined as the West Midlands, stretching
from Shrewsbury and Stafford in the north, to
Nuneaton and Coventry in the east, through
Leamington Spa and Honeybourne to Cheltenham
in the south, and encompassing Hereford in the
west.

The purist might cavil at the inclusion of such
distant county and country towns in a 'West
Midlands' area, but all have services which in one
way or another relate to the electrified main line.
Historically, Birmingham was the objective of the
London & Birmingham Railway from Euston, and of
the Grand Junction Railway from the north.
Amalgamating to form the nucleus of the London &
North Western Railway in 1846, these routes
together with the Trent Valley line of 1847 are
arguably the busiest and most important trunk
railways in the country.

Whatever differences may have arisen between
the LNWR and the Midland Railway elsewhere, in
Birmingham their interests were complementary.
Thus an early agreement to share passenger facilities
at New Street station was reached, and the
Midland's penetration from Derby through to Bristol
via Bromsgrove created another major rail route to
serve Britain's second city. The coming of the Great
Western Railway was a less harmonious affair. For
one thing it was broad (or at least mixed) gauge; for
another it directly threatened the interests of Euston,

both for traffic to London and to Liverpool via Birkenhead. So began a series of undignified skirmishes which led to a riot at Wolverhampton in 1850 and a display of force two years later. So the GWR, through its purchases of lesser companies in the area, developed as a separate railway system.

For perhaps a century, the three companies (reduced to two by the absorption of both the LNWR and the Midland into the London Midland & Scottish Railway in 1923) served the area well. One positive gain was the number of alternative routes which became available through the piecemeal development of the system, engendered in part by the competitive environment. But the 1950s brought a change; no longer could a system unified now as British Railways attract as much traffic as was needed to sustain all the competing trunk routes which were then still in existence. Although it was not acknowledged at the time, the Modernisation Plan decision to electrify the former LNWR routes spelt the beginning of the end for the old GWR system.

For a few years, the Western Region lines enjoyed an enhanced service while engineering work played havoc with services elsewhere. The highlight was the introduction of the luxury Blue Pullmans in 1960, which ran from Paddington to Wolverhampton Low Level, calling intermediately at Leamington Spa, Solihull and Birmingham Snow Hill. They did it rather quicker in a British Transport Film, made to replace 'London to Brighton in Four Minutes'! But electrification brought the Pullmans to an end, and with them Snow Hill as a main line station. New curves at Bordesley, Smethwick and Wolverhampton connected what remained of the ex-GWR empire to the metals radiating from New Street; from Banbury northwards it had been within the London Midland

Region since 1963. Since then the process has continued; Euston-Birmingham is now a half-hourly InterCity service, whereas the remaining trains entering the area via Leamington Spa tend to originate in places like Brighton, Portsmouth and Poole rather than Paddington. Even Worcester may now be reached from London via Birmingham in 2hr 43min, only 25min slower than the best timings via the now downgraded but far shorter Cotswold line.

While the electric services have maintained their standards, the introduction of Inter-City 125s on the old Midland North East-South West route has at long last provided a welcome fillip to British Rail's premier cross-country line. Although there is no scope for 125mile/h running in the West Midlands area, the greater acceleration and smarter journey times, together with the public appeal of these units, has provided the most notable improvement to West Midlands InterCity services in recent years.

Such are the bare bones of the history of the main routes; the development of freight and the local passenger services, some under the energetic guidance of the West Midlands Passenger Transport Executive, is described within. To those wishing to know more of the history I can do no better than to refer them to Rex Christiansen's *The West Midlands* and *Thames and Severn*, volumes 7 and 13 respectively in *The Regional History of the Railways of Great Britain* published by David & Charles. As usual, I am indebted to my photographic contributors, whose work has greatly enhanced this volume. Their names appear with the appropriate captions; the remaining uncredited pictures are my own.

John Glover
Ewell, Surrey
September 1983

Electric InterCity

Despite all the huffing and puffing on the desirability of electric traction, the Euston/Birmingham/ Manchester/Liverpool (EBML) electrification of 1966/67 and its 1974 extension to Glasgow remains Britain's only true main line electrified railway. The Trent Valley line, one of the earliest examples of a cut-off (it reduced the Rugby-Stafford distance by eight miles when it opened in 1847), went electric in April 1966 and thus preceded the Birmingham area by 11 months. Electric locomotives with 100mile/h capability were provided together with the earliest examples of 100mile/h Mark II coaching stock which, however, were vacuum braked. The result was spectacular. As *Modern Railways* reported,

'Britain's first 80mile/h start-to-stop schedules are a highlight of the new service to be introduced on 18 April. It will be unsurpassed in the Western world for a combination of speed and regular interval frequency'. 1967 saw the introduction of a standard 94min timing between Euston and Birmingham New Street, inclusive of the stop at Coventry.

In the intervening period, service frequencies have been improved, particularly with the start of a half hourly service all day between Birmingham and London in 1972. Air-conditioned versions of the Mark II coach were introduced at the same time, and locomotive-hauled Mark III vehicles made their

debut on the West Coast main line five years later. Although the fastest timings to Birmingham had improved to a 90min schedule, the 1983/84 best is again 94min, inclusive now of a stop at Birmingham International as well as Coventry. Journey times in general have thus not advanced, whereas elsewhere in this country and overseas the availability of 125mile/h trains has resulted in the London Midland Region's prime service looking a little tarnished:

Best Journey Times and Speeds from London to selected destinations 1983/84

London to:	Distance (miles)	Best time (min)	Av speed (mile/h)
Bristol Parkway	111¾	68	99
Doncaster	156	96	98
Coventry	94	66	86
Stafford	133½	94	85
Birmingham International	104¾	77	82
Nuneaton	97	72	81
Birmingham New Street	113¾	94	72
Wolverhampton	126	113	67
Bournemouth	108	98	66
Worcester Shrub Hill	120½	138	52

The clear superiority of the InterCity 125 services is marked, and it is interesting to see that the 90mile/h restricted Southern Region provides Bournemouth with almost as fast a service as Euston does for Wolverhampton. The poor relation position of Worcester may also be noted. The LMR's ac lines services may thus be seen to do little better than stagnate; whether the cost of investing to improve journey times is justified in view of cut price coach competition is one of the problems currently facing British Rail business managers.

The running of through services between Euston and stations north of Crewe via Birmingham is limited to two-hourly projections to Manchester, Blackpool or Holyhead, and the morning 'Clansman' to Inverness. Wolverhampton has a through hourly service from Euston throughout the day, but intermediate trains terminate at Birmingham. Other trains running north of New Street either start at Birmingham or arrive from origins away from the electrified network. Thus there are services such as the 06.45 Paddington-Edinburgh/Glasgow which provide scope for many intermediate journeys without a change, where historically no through facility had ever previously existed. Along the Trent Valley only Nuneaton and Stafford have a regular InterCity service; Tamworth and Lichfield have a token InterCity presence only.

Left: It is by no means unusual to see the earlier AC electric locomotives on express passenger duties. Doncaster built Class 85 No 85.027 hurries the predominantly Mark III stock of the 16.13 Manchester Piccadilly-London Euston through the centre roads of Stafford on 1 June 1982.

Above right: The unstaffed station at Rugeley offers the intending passenger only a couple of shelters. Un-named No 86.237 speeds past the up platform with the 10.21 Holyhead-London Euston on 2 June 1982.

Below right: Power signalboxes covering large geographical areas were out of favour when electrification was extended south from Crewe. Although the driver has the benefit of multiple signalling throughout, it is controlled from the original LNWR boxes as seen here at Polesworth on 21 October 1981. Class 87 No 87.023 *Highland Chieftain* is approaching on an unidentified up express. *John Whitehouse*

Above: Lichfield Trent Valley station is situated way out of the town centre. At one time passenger trains called here on the Lichfield City-Wichnor Junction-Derby high level line, but there are no booked passenger trains by this route nowadays. One of the high level platforms is still in use, acting as the bridge between the down and up sides of the low level station. Class 86/2 No 86.209 *City of Coventry* is heading the 11.25 Liverpool Lime Street-London Euston on 2 June 1982.

Below: An unidentified Class 85 locomotive approaches Nuneaton with an up express on 27 March 1982. The flyover in the background carries the Leicester-Birmingham freight line; passenger trains are routed via the Trent Valley platforms. There is a power signalbox here, the box on the left being no longer operational.

Above right: Entering Coventry on 31 May 1982 is the 14.30 Wolverhampton-London Euston, on time at 15.09. The locomotive is No 87.012 *Coeur de Lion*. Unauthorised access to or exit from the station is prevented here by a formidable steel fence seen to the right of the picture, which must be all of 9ft high.

Below right: No 85.027 leaves Coventry for Birmingham with the late running 13.10 train from London Euston on 31 May 1982. On the right Class 310 unit No 050 patiently awaits departure with the 14.32 all stations service to New Street.

Below: Birmingham International's prime purpose in life is to serve the adjacent National Exhibition Centre, although Elmdon Airport is also nearby and is being connected to the station by MAGLEV. This is an automatic unmanned transit system developed by British Rail in conjunction with the People Mover Group and working with the West Midlands County Council. On 31 May 1982 Class 87 No 87.003 *Patriot* is arriving with the 16.18 Birmingham New Street-London Euston.

Left: Class 86/2 No 86.213, now *Lancashire Witch,* traverses the cutting to the east of Lea Hall station on 4 April 1980 with the 11.30 Wolverhampton-London Euston. *Philip Hawkins*

Below: An unidentified Class 82 locomotive, one of the Metropolitan-Vickers machines based at Longsight Manchester, passes Adderley Park with a short train of Mark I rolling stock en route for London Euston on 2 May 1980. The tallest building in the background is Birmingham's British Telecom Tower, which can also be seen in four other pictures in this volume. *Les Nixon*

Right: On 22 March 1980 a Class 86/2 locomotive leaves the tunnels of central Birmingham behind as it gathers speed out of New Street with a London-bound express.

Below: This unbeautiful scene shows No 86.233 *Sir Lawrence Olivier* leaving Birmingham on the Stour Valley route to Wolverhampton with the 09.20 Brighton-Manchester Piccadilly on 5 June 1982. 15min is allowed for the change from diesel to electric traction at New Street on this service.

Above left: Class 86/2 No 86.227 *Sir Henry Johnson* passes Soho with an up express on the summer Saturday of 5 June 1982. The area is a crossroads for canals as well as railways; this is the Birmingham Canal.

Below left: No 86.214 *Sans Pareil* was finished in the new standard (?) livery in 1980 to mark 150 years of the Liverpool & Manchester Railway. A special commemorative panel was incorporated in the locomotive's side. It is seen near Smethwick on 5 June 1982 with the 09.40 Shrewsbury-London Euston. There seems to be a marked reluctance to turn out further AC electric locomotives in this paint scheme.

Above: English Electric built Class 83 No 83.012 provides assistance to sister locomotive No 83.019 which had failed while working the 16.25 Manchester Piccadilly-Cardiff Central on 29 May 1982. The pair, running very late, are approaching Smethwick Rolfe Street.

Right: Class 87 No 87.014 *Knight of the Thistle* approaches the site of Spon Lane station on 5 June 1982 with the 09.00 Wolverhampton-London Euston. In the background is the elevated M5 Motorway.

Above left: The 15.10 London Euston-Shrewsbury passes the narrow island platform of Dudley Port, alongside the Birmingham Canal. The locomotive is No 86.244 *Glenfiddich* and the date 4 June 1982.

Below left: At Wolverhampton, through trains to and from Shrewsbury exchange locomotives. This is the 07.40 Shrewsbury-London Euston on 14 April 1982. No 86.221 *Vesta* is backing on to the train, ready for a right time departure of 08.30.

Right: Class 87 No 87.008 *City of Liverpool* arrives at Wolverhampton with the 16.26 departure for Manchester Piccadilly. This train originated from Plymouth nearly five hours earlier at 11.38. The train spotters had by now gone home, leaving their unwelcome litter on the Post Office barrow.

Below: Class 83 No 83.007 leaves Wolverhampton for Stafford with the 12.50 London Paddington-Liverpool Lime Street on 1 June 1982. Situated a little to the north of the station, this landscaped area is a fine point from which to observe the passing transport scene.

InterCity on the North East-South West

North East-South West is a clumsy name, and although it is widely understood within British Rail it is far from clear to the average passenger where the service starts and where it finishes. Indeed the route itself is unspecified in the name, and one must have a certain sympathy with the staff who christened it the 'Heart Line' through large red letters painted on the ends of IC125 power cars upon the introduction of the accelerated HST timetable on 17 May 1982.

Unfortunately, 'Heart Line' is even less informative. The most precise definition is that all trains traverse the former Midland Railway line between Barnwood Junction, Gloucester, where the Bristol and South Wales lines converge, and run via Birmingham to Wath Road Junction, Mexborough, diverging again there for Leeds or York. (For some trains the divergence is at Altofts Junction, Normanton.)

The creation of the route was much influenced by railway politics. The original Birmingham & Derby Junction Railway's objective was to create a long since vanished link with the London & Birmingham at Hampton in Arden. With the completion of a more direct route from Derby to London, attention turned to Birmingham; the formation of the Midland Railway, the construction of New Street and the present route to King's Norton, and the acquisition of the Birmingham & Gloucester Railway from under the nose of the GWR resulted in the main line of today. The only engineering work of note (and how!) is the Lickey Incline, two miles of continuous 1 in 37 towards Birmingham. For years this constituted a major restriction on the line capacity, but dieselisation, track realignment and the elimination of the unfitted freight train has diminished its importance, although banking assistance is available continuously.

North of Birmingham, a later improvement was the opening of a cut-off between Water Orton and Kingsbury in 1909 to shorten the B&DJ route via Whitacre. Part of the original route is still used by the cross-country passenger link to Nuneaton, Leicester, Peterborough and Norwich.

Over the years, attempts have been made to achieve standard departure times of the NE-SW trains from New Street; in winter 1983 these were at 15min past the hour southbound and 50min past the hour northbound. A brief analysis of the northbound Monday to Friday timetable shows the complexity of the service pattern. Of the trains arriving on the hourly headway, nine originate from Bristol or points beyond, and one each from Cardiff Central and Swansea. A further five trains outside the basic service are from the West Country, and three more are from South Wales. Going forward at 00.50 or thereabouts, six trains are for York/Newcastle/Edinburgh and five for Leeds. One more train serves both routes by dividing at Sheffield, but three of the Leeds trains continue to York or beyond. At other times there is an additional York service, and an evening train terminates at Derby. No consistent pattern can be discerned in the timetable, but it is fair to say that connections are often available when no through train exists. A further complication is that some trains switch routes in the sense that four of the trains arriving via Bromsgrove continue after reversal on to the West Coast main line via Crewe and three terminate at New Street; conversely one of the trains going forward to Sheffield originates from

Poole and one is a Birmingham starter. Heavy weekend traffic is a feature of all these services, and relief trains are run for this purpose.

By comparison with the radial routes from London, the opportunity for really high speed running is strictly limited. Overall journey times are distinctly disappointing, and one might reasonably ask whether the BR tag of the 'Journey Shrinkers' is truly justified. Certainly the present timings are an improvement upon previous offerings, but comparison with the table in the previous section is painful when it is remembered that HST sets are in charge of all the principal services:

Best Journey Times and Speeds from Birmingham to selected destinations winter 1983/84

Birmingham to:	Distance (miles)	Best time (min)	Av speed (mile/h)
Newcastle	204	209	59
Leeds	116½	146	48
Sheffield	77½	79	59
Bristol Temple Meads	93½	80	70
Plymouth	221	200	66
Cardiff Central	110	109	61

Even allowing for the compulsory stop at Derby on all trains, a best speed of 59mile/h to Sheffield seems less than adequate. It must be hoped that further development and improvement of services on this major passenger route will be achievable in the years ahead.

Above: Approaching Water Orton on 3 June 1982 over the 1909 cut-off and with the cooling towers of Hams Hall power station in the background is No 45.148. The train is the 09.50 Newcastle/11.10 Leeds-Poole, which combined at Sheffield. The tracks to the right lead to Nuneaton.

Below: Water Orton station is maintained in spotless condition, and in 1982 it won the Birmingham Division's best-kept station award. HST set No 253.032 hurries through with the 09.18 Edinburgh-Penzance on the same day.

Above: Normally a DMU working, the 09.03 Cambridge-Birmingham New Street produced Class 31 No 31.270 and four coaches as it passed Washwood Heath gas works on 25 September 1982. *Geoff Dowling*

Above right: An IC125 set coasts down through Five Ways station towards New Street with the 07.55 Plymouth-Leeds on 29 May 1982. Five Ways was closed for 60 years before being reopened to passengers in 1978.

Below right: The Class 45 locomotives were associated with the North East-South West services for many years before the HSTs came on to the scene. No 45.012 passes the site of the old Somerset Road station with the 08.15 Plymouth-Leeds. *Geoff Dowling*

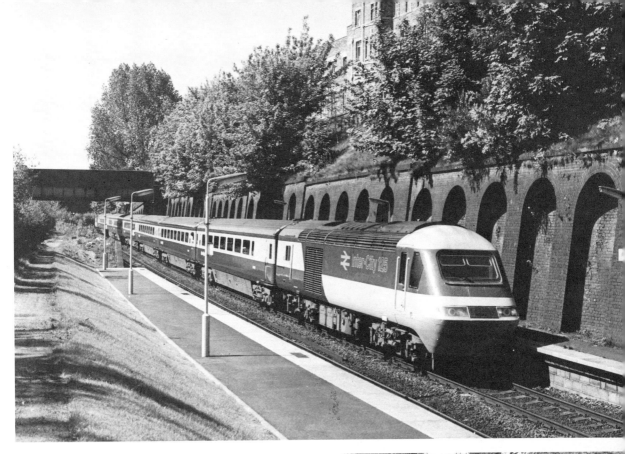

Left: The 10.23 Manchester Piccadilly-Plymouth with No 50.032 *Courageous* at its head is reflected in the still waters of the Birmingham Canal near University station on 24 March 1982. *Geoff Dowling*

Above: With HST power car No 43172 leading, the 14.32 Leeds-Swansea catches the last rays of the evening sun as it passes University on 25 September 1982. *Geoff Dowling*

Above left: Class 50 No 50.032 *Courageous* hurries the 13.20 Manchester Piccadilly-Taunton through Selly Oak on Saturday 29 May 1982. The architectural style is typical of the rebuilt stations on the Longbridge line.

Below left: A short seven-coach formation with Class 45/0 No 45.051 in charge approaches Barnt Green on 29 May 1982. To the right the lines diverge for the Redditch branch, but the express is heading for the top of the Lickey Incline.

Right: On 21 September 1982 the 07.40 Penzance-Liverpool Lime Street breasts the summit of the Lickey at Blackwell behind Class 47/4 No 47.450. *Brian Morrison*

Below: No 50.031 *Hood* descends the Lickey Incline at 70mph with the 09.20 Liverpool Lime Street-Penzance on 4 June 1982. The whole class is named after British warships, although some of the names used are those of naval shore bases.

Above: A 'Heart Line' HST passes the single platform of Bromsgrove station amid the oil storage tanks at the foot of the 1 in 37 incline. The train is the 07.55 Plymouth-Leeds, and on 4 June 1982 the unit was decorated with a large red heart below the windscreen!

Below: An unidentified Class 45/1 bound towards Cheltenham passes the pair of Class 37 banking locomotives Nos 37.267 and 37.255. In the background Class 31s Nos 31.276 and 31.153 have recently arrived with an oil train on 4 June 1982.

Right: There can be few places on British Rail where a set of block instruments is available for casual observation, but so it is at Wadborough Crossing, south of Abbots Wood Junction. Class 45/1 No 45.115 speeds past with the 08.25 Manchester Piccadilly-Cardiff Central. *Geoff Dowling*

Below: No 47.508 *Great Britain* approaches Cheltenham with the 13.20 Liverpool Lime Street-Plymouth on 22 March 1982. In the background may be seen the privately owned Coal Concentration Depot with its industrial diesel shunters. *Les Bertram*

Top: Class 50 No 50.041 *Bulwark* arrives at Cheltenham on 3 June 1982 with the 09.20 Liverpool Lime Street-Penzance. Formerly known as Lansdown, it is nowadays the only remaining railhead in Cheltenham.

Above: An HST set enters Cheltenham with the 07.55 Plymouth-Leeds on 3 June 1982. To the left of the picture can be seen the trackbed of the wholly GWR route to Birmingham via Honeybourne and Stratford-upon-Avon.

InterCity on the ex-Great Western Routes

The rail routes which suffered most in the process of rationalisation in the West Midlands have been those under the previous ownership of the Great Western Railway. With the loss of the London and Birkenhead traffics to the former LNWR routes, a new raison d'etre has had to be created for the routes which remain.

From the south approaching Birmingham via Leamington Spa, a completely new pattern of traffics has emerged. With through Paddington-Birmingham passengers of negligible importance, all but a solitary peak service have been diverted to run via Reading and Oxford rather than the pretty but sparsely populated route through Princes Risborough. However there is no shortage of Paddington-Reading-Oxford services, so the next step was to look for alternative originating points, even though some of these might mean reversal at Reading. North of Leamington, the construction of the National Exhibition Centre and the new station of Birmingham International was an ideal excuse to divert certain trains via the now single track link to Coventry and into Birmingham 'under the wires'. This of course made a corresponding reduction in the stops in the suburban centre of Solihull. (The Coventry-Leamington line was an LNWR branch, but has been included in this section as the services are more related to the GWR route.) The table indicates the variety of the services in winter 1983.

Ten trains run via Coventry, calling there and at Birmingham International, and three via Solihull. Paddington is still the originating point for five of the services, but the projection of the majority through to the WCML gives Thames Valley passengers a wide choice of destinations which can be reached by through services. Conversely,

passengers from the north of England are afforded access to Gatwick without going via London, although this usually means a change at Reading.

Shorn largely of its InterCity status is the Oxford, Worcester and Wolverhampton Railway, known as the 'Old Worse and Worse' in its past and perhaps in the present too. There are only two through London trains in each direction through Honeybourne to Worcester and thence to Hereford. These leave Hereford at 05.55 and 07.05, returning from London Paddington at 17.07 and 18.07. Hereford itself is as quickly reached via Newport; Worcester has alternatives via Gloucester and, as already remarked, via Birmingham. The outlook is not encouraging. The route has mostly been singled, although the long tunnels below the Malvern Hills and at Ledbury have always been single track.

Further north, the Wolverhampton-Shrewsbury section still thrives. It had always been a possibility that the Shrewsbury & Birmingham Company would form part of the LNWR empire, but political manoeuvrings of the 1850s ensured that it became

Northbound InterCity trains via Leamington Spa, Monday-Thursday, winter 1983/84

Paddington	—Manchester Piccadilly	1
	—Liverpool Lime Street	1
	—Wolverhampton	2
	—Glasgow Cen/Edinburgh	1
Brighton	—Manchester Piccadilly	2
Portsmouth Hbr	—Manchester Piccadilly	1
Poole	—Manchester Piccadilly	1
	—Liverpool Lime Street	2
	—Birmingham New Street	1
Total to AC lines		**12**
Poole	—Newcastle/Leeds	1
Total to NE-SW line		**1**

27

part of the GWR. Reconnection to the electric lines in 1967 caused no problems in itself, but Shrewsbury, reduced to a single through train to and from Euston, complained bitterly. Recasting of the electric timetable allowed more trains to be projected beyond Wolverhampton, and today there are three northbound and four southbound journeys on Mondays to Fridays. Electric locomotives are exchanged for (usually) a Class 47 diesel at Wolverhampton. The line passes through the New Town of Telford, but passengers have to use either Shifnal or Oakengates which are both served by the local services only.

Right: Class 47 No 47.455 passes All Saints' Parish Church at Leamington Spa as it leaves the station with the 10.34 Manchester Piccadilly-London Paddington on 31 May 1982.

Below: On Friday 11 January 1980 No 31.273 was the best that could be found for the 19.00 London Paddington-Manchester Piccadilly. The locomotive was however managing to keep time. On the right is the 21.00 local service for Stratford-upon-Avon. *G. O. Swain*

Top: No 50.014 *Warspite* approaches Hatton station at speed on 7 February 1981 with the 11.22 Liverpool Lime Street-London Paddington. Diverging to the left of the picture is the single track branch to Stratford-upon-Avon via Bearley. *Geoff Dowling*

Above: The 15.50 London Paddington-Birmingham New Street passes Bentley Heath, Dorridge, on 31 August 1981 behind No 47.476. All around can be seen evidence of the local 'industry' of the shipment of new Rover vehicles. *Geoff Dowling*

Above: Unrefurbished Class 50 No 50.011 *Centurion* leaves the remaining island platform at Solihull with the 08.35 Birmingham New Street-London Paddington on Spring Bank Holiday Monday, 31 May 1982.

Left: In its usual pristine appearance, No 47.511 *Thames* leaves Solihull with the 15.50 London Paddington-Birmingham New Street. To the left of the picture are the office block and bus interchange, both of which are built on the former goods yard site. This photograph was taken on 22 June 1981. *Geoff Dowling*

Above right: Small Heath Goods Yard, once very busy, now hardly exists. A raft of wagons for a scrap dealer with some Cartic 4s beyond are the sum total occupants on 30 May 1982, as No 50.016 *Barham* passes with the 08.25 Liverpool Lime Street-London Paddington. *Geoff Dowling*

Below right: No 47.168 joins the former Great Western line at Bordesley South Junction which it has reached via the Midland Camp Hill avoiding line, seen on the embankment in the background. The train is the 11.22 Liverpool Lime Street-London Paddington, photographed on 22 March 1980. *John Whitehouse*

Above left: The 16.23 Manchester Piccadilly-London Paddington train hauled by No 50.004 *St Vincent* has left New Street. It is seen here on 13 April 1981 passing alongside Landor Street, the main lorry route to the Freightliner terminal. *John Whitehouse*

Below left: On the route from Leamington Spa to Birmingham via Coventry, used nowadays by an increasing number of trains, Kenilworth station was once the pride of the line. Some of the grandeur can still be seen, but not the handsome glass lantern over the booking hall. The site is now a builder's yard. No 47.475 passes with the 09.20 Manchester Piccadilly-Poole on 23 January 1982. *Geoff Dowling*

Below: No 50.002 *Superb* leaves the electrified area at Coventry with the 13.26 Edinburgh/13.43 Glasgow Central-London Paddington on 27 July 1982 following a locomotive change. A Class 86/2 locomotive stands on the left. *John Whitehouse*

Right: Class 31 No 31.217 is seen between Lea Hall and Stechford on 3 August 1980 with a long train of Mark I coaching stock. The train is the 13.50 London Paddington-Liverpool Lime Street.

Left: Honeybourne station reopened for traffic on 25 May 1981 after 12 years closure, with merely a single platform. No 50.037 *Illustrious* is approaching on 24 April 1982 with the 16.03 Worcester Shrub Hill-London Paddington. *John Whitehouse*

Below: On the wet afternoon of 25 May 1981 at the well preserved Evesham station, No 50.049 *Defiance* stands with the 14.25 Worcester Shrub Hill-London Paddington. *Les Bertram*

Above right: Leaving Worcester Shrub Hill on 21 April 1981 with the 16.03 to London Paddington is No 50.026 *Indomitable*. GWR type lower quadrant signals are still well in evidence here.

Below right: Under the ridge of the Malvern Hills, No 50.016 *Barham* was photographed near Malvern Link on 16 May 1982 with the 16.30 Hereford-London Paddington. *John Whitehouse*

Left: The 16.30 Hereford-London Paddington is seen climbing out of the eastern portal of Ledbury tunnel. On the left are the remains of a siding intended to field runaway wagons, but surplus to requirements in these days of fully fitted freight trains. *Geoff Dowling*

Right: North of Wolverhampton, the line to Shrewsbury remains Great Western in appearances. Class 47/4 No 47.436 approaches Cosford at speed with the 09.40 Shrewsbury-London Euston on 1 June 1982.

Below: Entering Shifnal station on 1 June 1982 is No 47.503 with the 11.40 Shrewsbury-London Euston. The through London trains run non-stop between Wellington and Wolverhampton.

Above: 12 September 1981 saw Class 25/2 locomotives Nos 25.113 and 25.139 hauling the 10.07 Aberystwyth–London Euston as it arrived at Wellington. At one time this was a busy junction station, but only the main line remains today. *Brian Morrison*

Below: The Class 33 is now becoming a familiar sight on the Welsh borders. No 33.005 is in charge of the 11.50 Cardiff Central–Crewe, seen here arriving at Shrewsbury on 1 June 1982.

Commuter Services in the PTE

The area covered by the West Midlands Passenger Transport Executive is that of the Metropolitan County Council; its boundary is thus that of local government and therefore bears no direct relationship to the realities of public transport. Most of the built-up areas in the Coventry-Birmingham-Wolverhampton conurbation are included, and with them the local electric service and the route to Walsall. In all other cases a straggly bit is left outside the boundary. Thus the Lichfield line is covered as far as Blake Street, the Leamington line to Dorridge, the North Warwickshire to Earlswood, the Redditch service as far as Longbridge, and the Kidderminster line as far as Stourbridge Junction but including the short branch to Stourbridge Town.

The involvement of the PTE has restored the fortunes of the local rail services. In 1974/75 only 11.2million local journeys annually were being made on the entire rail network, and it might have been argued that continued financial support was not worthwhile. Fortunately, such an attitude did not prevail, and eight years later in 1981/82 passenger journeys had doubled to 22.5million. This was slightly lower than the high spot reached two years previously due, no doubt, to the economic recession.

How did this remarkable turnround come about? The PTE was not slow to recognise that proper integration of bus and rail services, with the former feeding into the latter at specially developed interchanges for the onward journey to the City Centre, was a desirable policy. Thus at Solihull a bus terminal was constructed on the site of the old goods yard; others have been developed at Marston Green and Northfield, for instance. Physical interchange has been backed up by the introduction of a combined ticket system, and the various Travelcards which give their holders within a geographical area automatically include rail as well as bus travel. For

regular travellers, there is thus no cost penalty in transferring between bus and train.

Car parking has also come in for attention: thus Four Oaks and Stourbridge Junction are but two stations which have had their car parks improved and extended. All the local railways have shown an increase in traffic, but the most gratifying result has come from the virtual reinstatement of the Longbridge service. The Passenger Transport Development Plan of 1972 identified the route as a prime target for upgrading and linking with the Lichfield line. From a residual service of four trains each way daily in 1975, 1979/80 saw an expanded service of over 70 trains on weekdays with an hourly Sunday service, and an explosion to 5.2million passengers. To achieve this, Five Ways was reopened and new stations were constructed at University and Longbridge; other stations along the route were completely rebuilt. Taken together with the Lichfield line, with which it is jointly operated, annual passenger carryings have more than trebled over the period. Less spectacularly, the Stourbridge line has been given a half-hourly service. Studies were taking place in 1982 to evaluate the benefits of a new — or should it be a reincarnated — Cross-City link between Stourbridge and the Leamington/North Warwickshire routes via Snow Hill. Implementation of this scheme would make Moor Street surplus to requirements, but the main disadvantage would be the reduction of direct access to New Street for InterCity connections.

Despite the undoubted successes, rail has an uphill struggle in front of it in the West Midlands. Buses still account for 96% of all passenger journeys by public transport in the PTE area, although the longer average distance of rail journeys reduces the share of the bus when journey length is taken into account. Electrification of the principal services must be a serious option; Longbridge would be included automatically in a North East-South West main line scheme, and catenary exists as far as Aston on the Lichfield route already. Diesel multiple-unit replacement is becoming urgent, and it is perhaps significant that public trials of the superior Class 210 units commenced on the PTE's Cross-City service.

Right: One of the four Class 312/2 units No 312.201 leaves Stechford on 3 August 1980 with the 15.21 all stations Birmingham New Street-Coventry. These units were built specifically to enable service frequencies to be improved.

Below: Class 304 unit No 024 will bounce anybody who cares to try it all stations except two from Birmingham New Street to Manchester Piccadilly. On 4 August 1980 the 17.21 from New Street calls at Smethwick Rolfe Street.

Above: Near Dudley Port on 4 June 1982, a Class 304 unit is seen alongside the canal with an evening all-stations commuter trip from Birmingham New Street to Wolverhampton.

Below: The 08.33 Wolverhampton-Birmingham New Street starts its journey on 14 April 1982. Passengers on the down platform are awaiting a special excursion to Edinburgh.

Above left: Class 304 No 304.008 was photographed in Platform 2 of the modern station at Wolverhampton on 1 June 1982. It will shortly be forming the 16.05 local service to Birmingham New Street.

Below left: Class 312/2 unit No 312.204 leaves Duddeston with the 16.25 Walsall-Birmingham New Street on 29 May 1982. On the right Class 08 shunter No 08.920 awaits its next duty outside the adjacent carriage sheds.

Right: No 310.081 arrives at Bescot on 3 June 1982. The train is the 16.12 Birmingham New Street-Walsall. The beginnings of Bescot yard can just be seen in the distance.

Below: The 16.54 from Walsall to Birmingham New Street enters Bescot; the destination blind is in error. The standard array of two headlight markers had been fitted to this end; for some reason the other end of unit No 310.081 has three.

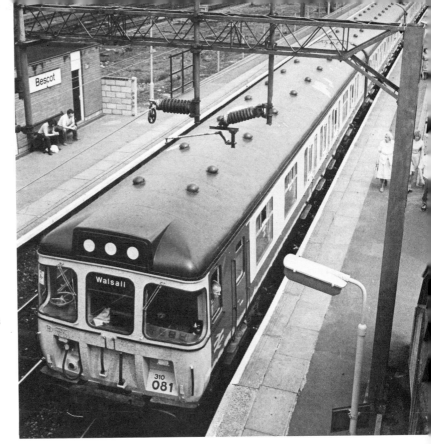

Above left: Walsall station has been redeveloped, although the facilities required for the limited passenger service are minimal. Unit No 312.203 awaits departure time for its return journey to Birmingham New Street on the sunny evening of 3 June 1982.

Below left: Three out of four trains on the Cross City line off-peak use Four Oaks as their northern terminus. The exception is the hourly service to and from Lichfield, and the 11.02 Lichfield City-Longbridge is seen arriving on 2 June 1982. The ticket office is worthy of especial note, with its lean-to greenhouse sheltering the passengers from the elements while business is being transacted.

Below: Arriving at Four Oaks is the 10.29 Longbridge-Lichfield City formed out of one of the ubiquitous Class 116 diesel-mechanical units on 2 June 1982. This line has LNWR origins, as the neat signalbox might suggest.

Right: A six-car formation of Class 116 units is being used for the 09.50 Longbridge-Four Oaks, which is pausing for a few minutes at Gravelly Hill on 2 June 1982.

Above left: Gravelly Hill interchange or Spaghetti Junction in popular parlance is a remarkable tangle of motorway intersections. However, the canal got there first, and the railway soon followed. Both were circumnavigated by the roadbuilders, and a Lichfield City-Longbridge train threads its way through the concrete pillars in March 1980.

Below left: Class 25 No 25.285 bound for Duddeston Sidings with some empty stock was caught at Aston by a signal failure on 29 May 1982. As a result, the approaching DMU for Lichfield City was unable to proceed beyond the station as the Class 25's train was fouling the junction for the branch; nearly an hour's delay ensued.

Above: The smart appearance of Five Ways is enhanced by a clean train and bright sunlight. The 09.50 Four Oaks-Redditch is seen leaving on 29 May 1982.

Right: Tyseley has one or two scratch sets! Here a Class 100 Gloucester unit composed of two power cars Nos M51110/9 and a Class 101 Metro-Cammell trailer in between arrive at University with the 10.02 Lichfield City-Longbridge on 29 May 1982.

Left: The Class 210 diesel-electric prototype multiple-units made their debut on the Cross-City line. No 210.002 leaves University on 2 October 1982 with the 11.50 Four Oaks-Longbridge. *Geoff Dowling*

Below: Stourbridge Town sation must be the smallest on British Rail, with the capacity to hold only a single unit diesel since the remainder of the station was demolished in order to enlarge the bus terminal. A Class 122 unit arrives on the shuttle from Stourbridge Junction on 4 August 1980.

Right: The branch climbs steeply from Stourbridge Town, but even so a fixed distant is provided on the approach to the Junction. The line is only $\frac{3}{4}$-mile long, and the journey time is three minutes.

Above: Class 122 Gloucester built Driving Motor Brake Second No M55009 approaches Stourbridge Junction on the evening of 23 October 1982. The timetable lays down 64 journeys in each direction daily, but the service is amended 'as circumstances require'.

Below: A break between trips at Stourbridge Junction enables the train crew to enjoy the evening sun. This photograph was taken on 29 May 1982.

Above: A calling on arm is in use as the 09.30 Birmingham New Street-Stourbridge Jucntion passes Rood End Yard near Langley Green on 2 June 1982.

Below: The 08.10 Kidderminster-Birmingham New Street leaves Smethwick West on 5 June 1982. The line in the foreground now leads to Handsworth only, the tracks thence to Snow Hill having been lifted. The catch points from the branch seem to be of little value, since any rolling stock caught by them would stand a good change of obstructing the main lines.

Left: 'You dash into the tunnel very fast, and the brakes go on, and you look out of the window and all down the tunnel at intervals are a lot of flare lights, and in between these flare lights are men, standing . . .' Thus Reginald Gardiner, half a century ago. The picture shows Snow Hill station site as it was on 23 October 1982, with the abandoned tunnels still there but buildings and platforms reduced to nothing more than a car park. If present plans come to fruition, a new station might yet arise on the site with one tunnel put back into use.

Below: Moor Street station is a compact three platformed terminus. On 22 March 1980, local services to Stratford-upon-Avon and Leamington Spa are in evidence.

Right: The Class 140 prototype diesel unit ran trials on the Moor Street lines for a four week period. It is seen here crossing Bordesley viaduct on the last trip of the day with the 18.41 Birmingham Moor Street-Stratford-upon-Avon on 30 July 1981.

Above: A Birmingham panorama from Bordesley station on 3 January 1981 sees the 11.43 Birmingham Moor Street-Shirley approaching. To the right of the picture is the track bed of the former main lines to Snow Hill.
Geoff Dowling

Left: Class 140 unit No 140.001 arrives at Small Heath with the 11.50 Birmingham Moor Street-Shirley on 30 July 1981. This picture gives little indication of the extent by which services in the area had been reduced and track formations rationalised.

Top right: For the Royal Wedding of 1981, Tyseley specially prepared a Class 116 DMU in the original refurbished livery and decorated it with flags. It is seen here leaving Tyseley for Birmingham Moor Street with the 11.02 local service from Dorridge on 30 July.

Centre right: Commuters heave a sigh of relief as they leave their Class 101 Metro-Cammell diesel unit at Wythall on 30 July 1981. The train is the 17.25 Birmingham Moor Street-Henley-in-Arden.

Below right: On 31 May 1982 a Class 116 unit calls at Dorridge with the 09.28 Leamington Spa to Birmingham. Normally, local services terminate at Moor Street, but being a Bank Holiday Moor Street is closed and an additional eight minutes will be spent gaining access to New Street instead.

Rural Services

West Midlands county is surrounded by Staffordshire, Warwickshire and Hereford and Worcester, while the greater part of the Shrewsbury route lies in Shropshire. The local rail services are a mixed bag, supported nationally under the Public Service Obligation and typified by the use of ageing DMUs and, in many cases, by unstaffed stations. Some routes are traversed by InterCity trains which do not stop anywhere in the area, the obvious example being the expresses on the Trent Valley line. Intermediate travel between Nuneaton and Stafford is catered for by an infrequent EMU service running six times in each direction on weekdays only. Similarly, on the Birmingham-Derby main line, the stations of Water Orton, Wilnecote and (even) Tamworth have but a sparse service of DMUs in contrast to the HSTs now in charge of the principal expresses. Other radial routes from Birmingham have more regular headways, being extensions of the PTE supported service to Lichfield City or Kidderminster, and to Leamington Spa and Stratford-upon-Avon. In this part of Warwickshire will be found one of the few remaining cross-country branches with single track, between Hatton and Bearley West Junction. It provides access to Stratford-upon-Avon from the south of England via Leamington Spa, but as far as London is concerned it is quicker to travel from Euston to Coventry and take the 'Shakespeare Connection' coach. 'There is no easier way of travelling . . . ' — quote from BR publicity.

One of the greatest problems has faced Hereford and Worcester County Council. Redditch New Town was originally intended to be within the West Midlands County Council area, and all the plans for the Longbridge service assumed that Redditch would be the terminus. The subsequent exclusion of Redditch from the metropolitan area left Longbridge as the end of PTE responsibility. The County Council has decided to sponsor an hourly train service to and from Redditch, but it was only in October 1982 that British Rail felt that they had a sufficiently long term commitment, and advertised the service in the timetable. Now passengers also have the benefit of also being able to use a special extended version of the West Midlands Travelcard, giving all the advantages of inclusive ticketing.

One of the more substantial service revisions has been the recent revamping of the Worcester area services. With the gradual running down of the Paddington-Worcester-Hereford line as a through route, and the replacement of most of the InterCity services north of Oxford by DMUs, has come the decision not to service Worcester by trains diverted from the Birmingham-Bristol main line. This has created the opportunity to provide a more regular Birmingham-Kidderminster-Worcester (-Hereford) link, together with DMU connections between Worcester and Cheltenham. For the time being at least, the proposal to create a new InterCity station where the Worcester-Oxford line crosses the NE-SW route is in abeyance.

For the non-InterCity and non-commuter services, the future is far from clear, and there is a suspicion in some circles that buses could do the job more efficiently and more cheaply. As British Rail's present Chairman has admitted, it is hard to see a long term future for railways in rural areas.

Above: The branch through Claverdon is again single track, having been doubled only in 1939. On Sunday 8 June 1980 a refurbished DMU with a blind reading 'Kettering for Corby' is passing with the 11.15 Stratford-upon-Avon-Leamington Spa. *Les Bertram*

Below: Bearley station (Halt according to the nameboards but not the timetable) sees the 12.31 Stratford-upon-Avon-Leamington Spa approaching on 31 May 1982. The station is used by only a handful of passengers.

Top: Unusually, the Stratford-upon-Avon–Leamington Spa shuttle was being worked by a pair of Class 122 single units on 30 July 1981. The train is seen in Platform 1 of Stratford-upon-Avon shortly after arrival. Once upon a time it would have been possible to continue to Honeybourne and Cheltenham, but the track now ends just beyond the overbridge.

Above: Wilmcote is an attractive and well preserved wayside station. It is seen here on 30 July 1981 with a train consisting of a Class 116 unit approaching from the North Warwickshire line.

Above: Leaving Wood End tunnel, a newly repainted Class 116 unit is forming the 15.11 Birmingham Moor Street-Henley-in-Arden on 30 July 1981.

Below: The minute station of The Lakes is approached by the experimental Class 140 unit No 140.001 on 30 July 1981 with the 16.11 Birmingham Moor Street-Stratford-upon-Avon. As can be seen by the positioning of the three-car marker on the up side, the platform capacity is limited to two vehicles.

Above left: The rebuilt Kidderminster station sees a healthy patronage awaiting the 09.35 departure for Birmingham New Street formed of a Class 101 unit with a Class 116 behind on 30 July 1981.

Below left: Hartlebury has only four weekday trains towards Worcester. A solitary passenger awaits the 13.00 Birmingham New Street-Worcester Foregate Street on 21 March 1980. The footbridge has since been demolished.

Above: A Class 101 unit arrives at Droitwich Spa on 4 June 1982 with the 08.30 Birmingham New Street-Hereford. The signalbox lies in the junction between the lines to Kidderminster and Bromsgrove.

Right: A Western Region based Class 101 unit leaves Worcester Shrub Hill on 3 June 1982 with the 09.05 Oxford-Hereford.

Top: With destination blind firmly suggesting the Welsh Valleys, a Class 119 Gloucester Cross Country three-car set arrives at Worcester Foregate Street with the 17.40 Hereford-Birmingham New Street on 21 April 1981. The tracks here are signalled bi-directionally, and from Platform 2 it is only possible for up trains to proceed towards Droitwich.

Above: A class 119 unit eases the 16.16 Worcester Shrub Hill-Hereford over the well known canal bridge on its descent to Foregate Street on 21 April 1981. Regrettably, patronage appears to be minimal.

Top: Crossing the River Severn at Worcester is a Class 116 unit on the same day; the train is the 17.03 Worcester Shrub Hill-Great Malvern.

Above: The 08.08 Hereford-Worcester Shrub Hill consisted of a Bristol area three-car Class 101 DMU on 21 April 1981. At that time, the train connected at Worcester with a locomotive hauled service to London Paddington.

Top: The remains of Colwall station see a Class 119 set arriving with the 10.30 Hereford-Worcester Shrub Hill. Single track now extends from Malvern Wells to Ledbury, although there was once a second platform here as can be seen.

Above: The 11.45 Worcester Shrub Hill-Hereford meets the 12.00 up train at Ledbury on 21 April 1981. In the background is the 1,323yd Ledbury tunnel.

Above: A pair of Swindon Cross Country Class 120 DMUs leave Billbrook with the 11.00 Shrewsbury-Wolverhampton on 17 April 1982. The station has staggered platforms, one on each side of the road overbridge.   *Geoff Dowling*

Below: At Codsall station, two people await the arrival of the 10.40 Wolverhampton-Shrewsbury formed of a Chester based two-car Class 101 Metro-Cammell set. *Geoff Dowling*

Above left: A Class 120 set arrives at Shifnal on 1 June 1982. The train is the 11.50 Wolverhampton-Chester. On the station building may be seen one of those fast disappearing notices, giving those paternalistic instructions so beloved of the GWR.

Below left: A Derby Lightweight set of Class 108 arrives at the commodious Wellington station with the 12.50 Wolverhampton-Shrewsbury on 1 June 1982.

Above: At Shrewsbury may be observed the Central Wales line DMUs formed out of Class 120 units reduced to a pair of driving motor vehicles and fitted with headlights. The 15.43 Shrewsbury-Swansea awaits departure from a south end bay.

Above right: Mid morning at Lichfield City on 2 June 1982 shows minimal activity apart from a Class 116 unit being stabled in the sidings.

Below right: Arriving at the up branch platforms at Barnt Green is the 13.24 Redditch-Four Oaks on 29 May 1982. Despite its four platforms the station is unstaffed; the main line platforms are used only by one train per day in each direction.

Left: The 11.24 Redditch-Four Oaks leaves the remote country station of Alvechurch on the winding Redditch branch on the same day. The station house is now privately occupied.

Above: Arriving at Alvechurch is the 10.50 Four Oaks-Redditch. There are exits in all directions; note particularly the sleeper crossing and the steps up the embankment on the left.

Right: Redditch station has been rebuilt on a new site as part of the New Town development. There is 22min turnround time allowed, and on pleasant days such as the afternoon of 29 May 1982 this allows the crews a chance to stretch their legs.

Above and below: The 08.55 Hereford-Birmingham New Street called at Bromsgrove on 4 June 1982. Formed of a Class 119 three-car unit it was well filled, and had a gross weight of perhaps 115 tons. Such considerations apparently required the use of the 3,500hp banking facilities provided by the pair of Class 37 diesels Nos 37.255 and 37.267, seen here giving a noisy push up the 1 in 37 of the Lickey Incline to the Cardiff based DMU.

Railfreight

In West Midlands as elsewhere, coal is the main freight traffic of British Rail. In Birmingham Division alone, well over 200 merry-go-round trains are run each week to and from collieries and power stations within and outside the area. Next in importance is oil, with about 120 weekly services. This is all received traffic, as there are no refineries within the Division. Iron and steel, cement, cars and chemicals are the other principal commodities carried. Economic stagnation has adversely affected the carryings of all traffics, especially in the construction industry; the Dudley Freightliner terminal just remains open, but most freightliner traffic is concentrated at Lawley Street,

Birmingham. For import/export traffic, the facilities of the Inland Port at Landor Street are available.

The principal marshalling yard is at Bescot, neatly situated on the electrified Grand Junction route but with good access to and from the ex-GWR and Midland lines. A motive power depot is nearby, and local trip working is provided by its stud of Class 25 Bo-Bo locomotives. Some mileage of freight-only lines is maintained so that Bescot may be reached, but these also enable freight trains to avoid the centre of Birmingham, and New Street in particular.

Below: A Freightliner from Dudley to Glasgow passes Hamstead station behind Class 87 No 87.013 *John o' Gaunt* in July 1980. *John Whitehouse*

Above left: A Scottish based locomotive No 81.016 passes Stafford heading north with a train of Ford parts for Halewood on 1 June 1982.

Below left: Most powerful locomotives on British Rail in 1982 were the Class 56s. No 56.102, one of the new liveried examples, is seen near Water Orton with a merry-go-round coal train on 4 June 1982.

Above: Between Leamington Spa and Warwick, Class 56 No 56.047 hurries some empty mgr hoppers from Didcot along the former GWR main line on 11 April 1981. *Brian Morrison*

Right: On Hatton bank, No 56.091 is in charge of a trainload of empties on 17 June 1982. The 3,250hp of these machines gives an appreciable increase in haulage capacity compared with the Class 47 locomotives they displaced from this work. *Geoff Dowling*

Above: Class 47/0 No 47.186 approaches Stechford on 3 August 1980 with a well loaded Freightliner bound for Lawley Street.

Left: Hereford sees plenty of freight activity, with trains routed through the lines between the platforms to allow passenger traffic to take precedence. On 21 April 1981, Class 47 locomotives No 47.187 and No 47.240 are in charge of northbound and southbound trains respectively, seen here to the north of the station.

Above right: Big locomotive, little traffic! On 4 June 1982 Class 46 No 46.016 approaches Droitwich Spa from the Kidderminster direction with what at first the photographer mistook for a light engine working.

Below right: Class 44 locomotive No 44.004 in green livery and carrying its original number of D4 and name *Great Gable*, prepares to run round the 11.53 Toton-Rugby coal train at Nuneaton on 28 November 1980. *G. Scott Lowe*

Left: Langley Green station on 2 June 1982 sees Class 40 No 40.004 following a DMU slowly towards Birmingham with a train of tanks. On the right is the remains of the West Bromwich branch, leading now to a chemical works only.

Top right: No 40.136 leaves Worcester with a southbound tank train. On the right are the private sidings owned by Metal Box.   *Les Bertram*

Centre right: An indication of the condition of the British steel industry is provided in this view of the Wolverhampton Steel Terminal on 28 September 1982, with Class 40 No 40.099 in charge of some ferry wagons.   *Peter Shoesmith*

Below: Passing Hartlebury on 21 March 1980 is a Class 37 with a train of steel scrap. The Severn Valley Line used to commence here, but the junction has now been lifted.

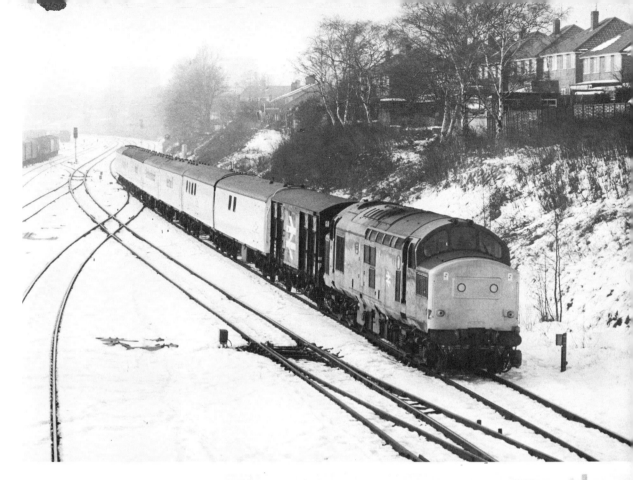

Above left: Trains leaving Bescot for Derby proceed by way of Lichfield City. Class 37 No 37.140 of March is hauling a northbound mixed freight on 2 June 1982.

Below left: On the misty 15 October 1980, No 37.211 heads towards Birmingham with a long oil train near Smethwick Rolfe Street. *Geoff Dowling*

Above: 'Salestrack '81' was a travelling exhibition train which spent a few days at selected stations around the country. On 24 February 1981 it was photographed taking the Birmingham line at King's Norton behind No 37.256. *John Whitehouse*

Right: Southern Region locomotives Nos 33.063 and 33.049 stand at Langley Green on 13 August 1980 having arrived from Southampton with a cement train, which they will run round before departing for the Handsworth terminal. *Geoff Dowling*

Above left: Class 31 locomotives Nos 31.276 and 31.153 with empty oil tanks return to the North East on 4 June 1982. They are being overtaken at Water Orton by an unidentified Class 45/1 with the 15.28 FO Birmingham New Street-York.

Below left: A pair of Class 25 locomotives headed by No 25.101 were trailing a long coal train as they arrived on the up side at Nuneaton on 27 March 1982.

Above: No 25.233 with a train of empty bogie bolsters passes Lichfield City in June 1980. The train is a Bescot-Toton working. *Geoff Dowling*

Above right: No 47.332 stands at Stourbridge Junction awaiting a possible banking duty towards either Bescot or Langley Green. Meanwhile, Class 25 No 25.276 is passing with a freight on 4 August 1980.

Right: Class 25 No 25.260 passes Bescot on 3 June 1982 with a parcels train from the Walsall direction.

Above: A pair of Class 25 locomotives, Nos 25.251 and 25.265 with two sets of Freightliner wagons storm through Water Orton on the afternoon of 4 June 1982.

Below: A mixed freight behind Class 20 locomotives Nos 20.043 and 20.063 is caught in the evening sun as it enters Washwood Heath sidings at Saltley Trading Estate on 23 August 1980. *Geoff Dowling*

Above: Two pallet vans behind a pair of Class 20s proceed at a smart pace through Birmingham International on 5 June 1980. *Peter Shoesmith*

Below: Under the M6 Motorway, Class 08 No 08.597 of Saltley shunts the Esso sidings at Bromford Bridge on 4 June 1982.

Top: No 08.700 is kept busy at Bescot, seen here on 3 June 1982 shunting an air braked long wheelbased wagon.

Above: When rolling stock has been condemned, it will usually be sold as scrap to a dealer and moved as freight to a scrapyard. Four vehicles from Eastern Region Class 306 stock dating from 1949 repose in the goods yard at Kidderminster on 3 June 1982, awaiting removal to their final destination.

Maintaining the Railway

There are many activities which need to be carried out by the railway which are not revenue earning in their own right. Maintenance of the rolling stock and the permanent way are activities which perhaps most readily come to mind; indeed, sometimes it seems that the Civil Engineer produces more 'freight' traffic than the paying customers! Other non-earning trains may be run for such diverse purposes as driver route learning, research, and attendance at accidents.

Perhaps the most surprising feature of the West Midlands scene is the lack of motive power allocation. The projected District Electric Depot at Soho, Birmingham, was never built, and multiple unit stabling there is the only function carried out for electric traction. Bescot Motive Power Depot has an allocation of only 86 locomotives made up of Classes 08, 25 and various subclasses of the 47s.

Although often host of visiting locomotives, Saltley residents are merely 13 Class 08 shunters. Tyseley also has three Class 08s, but its main purpose is to maintain the members of diesel multiple-unit classes 101, 116, 122 and sundry oddments allocated there. In the Western Region area, neither Hereford nor Worcester have any present day allocation. With the closure of Duddeston, Wolverhampton Oxley becomes the only servicing point for locomotive hauled coaching stock. Even British Rail Engineering Ltd has no workshops in the area, although Crewe, Derby, Wolverton and Swindon are all relatively close at hand.

Below: Class 40 No 40.181 passes slowly through Shrewsbury with a northbound train of ballast hoppers on 1 June 1982.

Above: A rare sight at Leamington Spa is Class 45/0 No 45.003 with an engineer's train heading south over the viaduct on 30 August 1980.
Geoff Dowling

Left: No 45.038 trundles through Butlers Lane with a ballast train on 19 September 1982.
John Whitehouse

Right: At the site of Rowington water troughs near Lapworth, No 25.262 works a permanent way train towards Warwick on 27 June 1981.
Geoff Dowling

Above: A ballast train passes Tamworth on the up slow line in the charge of Class 86/0 No 86.037 on 2 June 1982. As can be seen by the jumper cables, this is one of the class fitted for multiple working.

Left: 1953 built Ruston & Hornsby diesel shunter No PWM654 (now No 97.654) is based at Newland, near Worcester. On Saturday 13 February 1982, it was photographed at Honeybourne with a track relaying train for use on the following day.
Geoff Dowling

Right: 19 June 1982 saw No 31.214 at Hall Green with the Saltley Tool Vans en route for Stratford-upon-Avon to rerail an excursion train, which had become derailed in the goods loop.
Geoff Dowling

Above left: Duddeston Carriage Sidings are now closed, but on 29 May 1982 Class 87 No 87.009 *City of Birmingham* had arrived in the station platform with the empty stock of the 11.06 Edinburgh/11.15 Glasgow Central-Birmingham New Street. In this picture, the coaches are being drawn off the locomotive by the depot shunter, to be placed in the carriage shed.

Below left: Empty stock workings may be necessary, but do not earn revenue. No 50.003 *Superb* swings towards Birmingham New Street at Smethwick West Junction with empty stock from Worcester on 23 March 1982; it will form the 14.38 to London Paddington. There are no booked locomotive hauled passenger trains over this line.
Geoff Dowling

Right: No 50.008 *Thunderer* was photographed approaching Droitwich Spa with the same empty stock train a few weeks later, on 1 May 1982.
Geoff Dowling

Below: Worcester Stabling Point can be seen in the right background occupied by a Class 31 and some DMUs. In the foreground a Class 116 DMU has just left the depot and is preparing to take the route on the right to Foregate Street and form the 16.05 school train thence to Great Malvern on 21 March 1980. The Class 40 with empty bogie bolsters is heading towards Shrub Hill.

Left: Former Class 121 Pressed Steel unit No W55035, now No TDB975659, saunters through the site of Kings Heath station on the Camp Hill avoiding line on 13 October 1982. It is used for driver route learning purposes.   *Geoff Dowling*

Right: Drivers also have to be trained according to traction. Ex-Scottish Region Blue Train No 303.050 approaches Rugeley on the down line with a crew training special on 2 June 1982. The destination blind reads Liverpool Lime Street!

Below: Former Class 24 locomotive No 24.061 has been taken into Departmental stock as No 97.201, repainted in red and blue, and named *Experiment*. It is based at the Railway Technical Centre, Derby, and was photographed on 21 September 1982 ascending the Lickey Incline with a tribology section test train.
Brian Morrison

Excursions and Diversions

Nowadays, the thrust of British Rail's marketing policy is aimed at filling seats on timetabled trains that would otherwise be empty. The revenue thereby obtained is pure gain, and there are no train provision costs to be set against it. However, not all circumstances are relevant to the use of existing services; the Papal visit to Coventry for instance required a vast programme of extra trains at all hours of the day and night, to meet which DMUs were drafted in from as far away as Marylebone. The Merrymaker programme relies to some extent on special services through to destination, and may result in locomotive hauled trains on lines which normally only see multiple units. Similarly, privately chartered specials may be run wherever and whenever circumstances permit. If the charterer is a railway enthusiasts group, some truly remarkable scenes may be observed on occasion.

Other 'excursions' may be less welcome. The Civil Engineer has to do his work at some time, and in the West Midlands there is what almost amounts to an alternative network to the main passenger routes. If the Stour Valley line from Birmingham to Wolverhampton is not available, trains may be diverted via Bescot; if the route if blocked between Wolverhampton and Stafford, trains will be sent under diesel power via Hednesford to the Trent Valley line at Rugeley. Birmingham-Euston trains can be diverted via Nuneaton if the Coventry route is unavailable; for the NE-SW route via Tamworth read Lichfield City, and via King's Norton read Stourbridge Junction. There are many more alternatives available whether for planned or emergency use, and the net result is a limited need for replacement bus services at the expense of some elongated journey times.

Below left: Class 47/4 No 47.468 passes the closed Sutton Coldfield signalbox with a Wellington-York excursion on 3 October 1982. The train was subjected to diversion away from the normal route via Water Orton. *Geoff Dowling*

Right: The North Warwickshire line saw No 45.007 in charge of a Wooton Wawen-York charter train on the very wet morning of 20 June 1982. It is passing Shirley's remaining semaphore signals. *Geoff Dowling*

Below: A pair of Class 115 units borrowed from the Marylebone local services are seen on the Coventry-Nuneaton line on the occasion of the Papal visit to Coventry on 30 May 1982. The location is Three Spires Junction. *Geoff Dowling*

Left: Towards the end of the 'Deltics', many specials were run. The first (and last) appearance of the class in Birmingham took place on 28 November 1981. No 55.022 *Royal Scots Grey* passes Selly Oak on a Paddington bound special.
Geoff Dowling

Below: Until 1970, a Class 116 unit would have been an everyday sight at Bewdley, albeit not in the refurbished livery. On 20 April 1981 British Rail was running a through service between Kidderminster and Bewdley for the benefit of Severn Valley Railway patrons.

Above: The 10.18 SO Paignton-Manchester Piccadilly avoids Birmingham New Street altogether, being routed via Camp Hill, Castle Bromwich Junction, Walsall and Bushbury Junction. It was photographed passing the remains of Sutton Park station behind No 47.202 on 1 August 1981. *Geoff Dowling*

Below: The platforms of Whitacre station have been demolished and the track realigned. Here an IC125 set leaves the Nuneaton line bound for Birmingham New Street with the diverted 09.50 Newcastle-Plymouth on 27 June 1982. *Geoff Dowling*

Above left: On 6 September 1981 No 47.465 passes Hednesford goods yard with the southbound 08.25 Liverpool Lime Street-London Paddington. The wagons are stored out of use. *Geoff Dowling*

Below left: Class 47/4 No 47.557 climbs up the bank from Walsall to Bloxwich on 13 September 1981 with the 08.30 Birmingham New Street-Manchester Piccadilly. The now closed power station and waste ground are typical of the area.
Geoff Dowling

Right: Arriving at Wolverhampton on 14 April 1982 is Class 87 No 87.008 *City of Liverpool* with the 07.40 Birmingham New Street-Glasgow Central. The train had been diverted via Bescot because of a points failure at Soho and is seen here regaining its booked route at Crane Street Junction.

Below: No 47.483 pilots No 87.017 *Iron Duke* out of Birmingham New Street past Washwood Heath with the 12.00 Wolverhampton-London Euston on 30 August 1981. This is a regular Sunday sight, with electric locomotives hauled to Nuneaton when engineering work closes the Coventry route.
Geoff Dowling

Birmingham New Street

The 12 platforms of New Street station, Birmingham, are the focal point of British Rail's passenger operations. From them a greater variety of destinations can be reached by direct train service than from any other station in the country; the services offered include both the Dundee-Penzance and the London Euston-Inverness (the 'Clansman') trains, British Rail's two most lengthy through services. A vast and uncounted interchange of passengers takes place between the 600+ daily trains, while upstairs at concourse level 50-70,000 people pass through the ticket barriers every 24 hours.

Incomprehensibly to present day eyes, the Grand Junction Railway chose to ignore Wolverhampton and Walsall, its route terminating alongside the London and Birmingham Railway at Curzon Street, east of the City. Curzon Street remains today as a parcels depot, but the potential benefits of a centrally sited through station became obvious. The construction of the Stour Valley route to Wolverhampton, linking with the GJR beyond at Bushbury Junction provided the opportunity, and New Street opened in 1854. Curzon Street had also been shared by what became the Midland Railway; construction of the present main line route via Five Ways to King's Norton enabled Midland trains to use the new station, again without reversal. This had the incidental but anomalous result that northbound trains towards Derby leave alongside southbound trains for Euston; similarly services for Wolverhampton parallel those for Bristol out of the station.

Excellent though the site of New Street was, its capacity quickly became a problem. In 1885 the station was rebuilt on its restricted site, but the difficulties continued. Badly damaged in World War II, its general condition became notorious. Complete rebuilding was undertaken as part of the electrification scheme for the LNWR lines; this eliminated all the bay platforms and increased the through platforms from 8 to 12. All the station facilities were constructed on a concrete deck over the platforms, and a further level above this formed part of the shopping centre. The result is not beautiful, but it works reasonably well; its most irritating feature from the passenger's point of view is the inability of the escalators and staircases to deal with peak loads, which can cause trains to be missed.

The present layout gives the operators much scope for swapping around platforms in times of crisis, although it is clearly undesirable to send passengers scurrying around the station after their trains. Every platform is available to and from the Wolverhampton line, and all except Nos 11 and 12 to and from Coventry. North East-South West trains may use Nos 8-12 to and from Derby, but in the Bristol direction Nos 5, 6 and 7 are also available. Local trains leave the station on one of the main lines.

During their time in the platforms, several trains have to change locomotives from diesel to electric traction or vice versa, and this adds to calls upon the track capacity. Sometimes the locomotive is attached on the opposite end of a train, as a Manchester-Plymouth working for instance needs to reverse at New Street. The whole station operation is overseen by New Street signalbox, situated at the west end of the station on the 'Midland' side. The availability of alternative routes means that freight usually keeps well clear of the area.

Right: Class 87 No 87.014 *Knight of the Thistle* leaves platform 4 of Birmingham New Street on 5 June 1982 with the 14.30 Wolverhampton-London Euston. In the background is the concrete raft and part of the shopping centre.

Below: From above and looking towards Wolverhampton, the constricted site of the station is only too apparent. A Class 304 unit is arriving on 23 October 1982.

Top: Class 86 No 86.230 has just arrived from London Euston on 22 March 1980.

Above: On 5 June 1982, No 85.040 leaves with the 10.00 Paignton-Manchester Piccadilly. On the right, Class 86/2 locomotive No 86.233 *Sir Lawrence Olivier* awaits its next duty.

Above: Class 45/1 No 45.125 leaves New Street on 5 June 1982 with the 14.50 service to Leeds watched by an admiring crowd.

Below: Before the arrival of the HSTs, Class 47s were in charge of the principal trains on the NE-SW route. No 47.532 and No 47.107 are both awaiting departure.

Top: Class 45 No 45.110 in a modified livery arrives at Birmingham New Street with an express from Bristol Temple Meads on 4 August 1980. In the background is Class 87 No 87.002 *Royal Sovereign* with a train for Liverpool Lime Street.

Above: A quiet moment sees a Class 101 diesel unit in blue livery at the London end of New Street station.

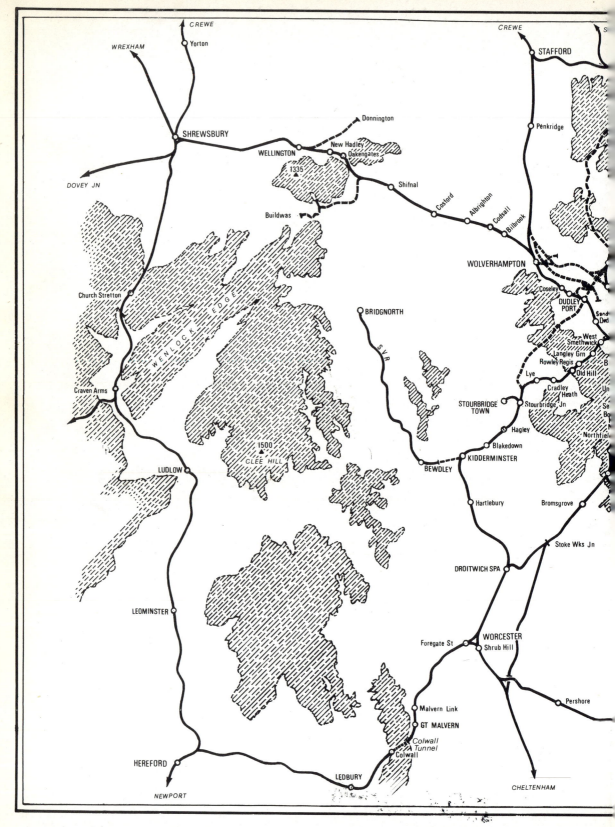